# The Journey From Darkness To Light

The Journey From Darkness To Light
Learn to Let Go, Transform & Heal Within
Rosie Kaur

All Rights Reserved. No portion of this book may be reproduced, stored in a retrieval system, or transmitted in any form or by any means-electronic, mechanical, photocopy, recording, scanning, or other-except for brief quotations in critical reviews or articles without the prior permission of the author.
Published by Game Changer Publishing
ISBN: 979-8-9851206-5-3

www.PublishABestSellingBook.com

# DEDICATION

*"One day you will tell your story of how
you overcame what you went through and
it will be someone else's survival guide"*

Dedicated to all my children who have supported
me and given me strength through the rough times. To my parents,
sis, family, and all friends around the world who crossed paths and
helped me on my journey of healing.

Especially to my brother Ace who was and is always there for me who
is my inspiration and motivation.

To my significant other thank you for your support
and everything you did and for shaping me into
the woman I am today!!!!

Dedicated to all the people of this world.
Wishing you Healing Within.

God bless. Love you all!

## DOWNLOAD YOUR FREE GIFTS

Just to say thanks for buying and reading my book, I would like to give you a few free bonus gifts, no strings attached!

### To Download Now, Visit:
http://www.healingwithrosie.com/freegift

# The Journey From Darkness To Light

Learn to Let Go, Transform & Heal Within

## Rosie Kaur

www.PublishABestSellingBook.com

# TABLE OF CONTENTS

Introduction ................................................................. ix
Overthinking ................................................................ 1
Let It Hurt Until It Can't Hurt Anymore ............................. 7
Life Is Getting up an Hour Early to Live an Hour More ........ 13
I'm Slowly Becoming the Person I Should
Have Become a Long Time Ago ...................................... 17
The Law of Attraction Is This—You Don't Attract
What You Want, You Attract What You Are.
Be the Person You Want to Attract! ................................. 21
You Make Your Life Hard by Always Being in Your Head.
Life Is Simple. Get Out of Your Head and Get
Into the Moment. .......................................................... 25
Forgiveness and Letting Go ............................................ 27
Some Journeys Take Us Far From Home &
Some Adventures Lead Us to Our Destiny ....................... 33
Conclusion & Resources ................................................ 35
About The Author ........................................................ 37
Testimonials ................................................................ 41
Thank You For Reading My Book! ................................ 43

# INTRODUCTION

As I sit here in my living room, gazing at the fireplace, I can reflect back on the events from just 4 short years ago. I had hit rock-bottom darkness before coming into light. I'd gone from full-blown panic and being suicidal to serenity and calmness.

Hi, my name is Rosie, and not so long ago, I was going through the worst years of my life. I wanted to end my life and commit suicide. It took rock-bottom darkness for me to have light within me and still, I remember those days trying to pray and all I had was brain fog. I felt that there were bricks on my head. There was no pain, but just extreme pressure. With big alligator tears rolling down my cheeks I said, "God you have taken everything from me? Please don't take my prayers away." At that time, I could see nothing (meaning the blessings in my life). My entire life was crashing all around me and I just felt that this was it. I was going to die and commit suicide. End my life. Everyone around me would say… "Save yourself, go to CMAH or talk with the Mental Crisis team." My glucose was through the roof and the doctors gave up on me. They didn't know what was going on. I still remember my family doctor saying, "The only thing normal in you is your blood pressure." Everything else is a mess and my doctors were giving up on me. I was sick of taking so many meds, insulin and all! They didn't help. It felt like the only thing it helped was shutting down my brain. The medication only suppressed my emotions and I couldn't even cry

## Introduction

and I felt drowsy all day. This is how it all started and where my anxiety turned into a major panic.

In September of 2019, my significant other left me without telling me, causing major panic attacks. It felt as if a part of my body was cut off. I started to feel as if there was a ball stuck in between my rib cage, similar to the xiphoid process (the small hard lump at the lower end of the sternum). It hurt so badly between my rib cage and upper stomach. I couldn't cook, eat, get up, or anything. I made sure my kids made it to school on time. I remained strong in the eyes of my kids. As soon as they left, I cried and felt like I had lost a major piece of my life. I couldn't get over it. My 1-year-old child was hungry, but all I had was a bottle of milk. I was so down. Down to the point, I started throwing away all my colored clothing, throwing away my furniture, decor and dishes in the house. It was bad. I had so much panic. I had pain in my spine. Like a ball going slowly up my spine and which would trigger a major panic attack. I drove for Uber then. One kid would come home so I could go to work and that child would watch the little baby. If I was late, I would get high anxiety. I would break pots, pans and vases, whatever came in my hand. I started getting worried. I thought I was going to kill one of my kids or myself. I had to tell the doctor what was happening.

I booked an appointment to see the doctor around mid-October. I went to see him… *What if he takes my kids away or puts me in a mental asylum?* I told him, "I need to share something with you. I am worried that you will send me somewhere or take my kids away."

He says, "Tell me what's wrong."

I told him, "I am worried that I am going to kill one of the kids or myself because my anxieties are getting bad." I told him I hadn't eaten in days. All I was having was chamomile tea. I told him about the pain in between my ribs… "It feels like a ball is stuck there. Also, before an episode arises I feel like something goes up my spine." He tells me it is definitely a panic attack. He prescribed me Lorazepam. This drug worked within 10 minutes of taking it. I loved it! I knew I needed more, but things still continue to go downhill. My relationship with my kids gets worse. I am constantly crying in bed and not able to get up, blaming everything on my significant other; that he left me with a mountain of baggage to carry around and deal with. I think I am being so positive. The only thing negative is me getting upset at the kids.

After this, every month around the same date something bad happens. I still do all my duties of picking up, dropping off all my children. Paying bills, mortgage, running the house, but I am crashing. I continue to find excuses to talk to my significant other, but all I get in return is conflict — I am dying. I literally feel like a rose dying and losing petals and drying up.

I am even more sick by December 2019. I start to throw up and still can't eat. I can no longer drink tea. I'm forcing myself to eat less than half a bowl of soup or half a glass of ginger ale. I get chills and stay in my room with three heaters on. I don't want to see anyone. I only wanted to hide from the public and family. I would feel if I came out to the light, people would point fingers and laugh at me and say, "Look at that lady. Her husband left her. She has so many kids." Yet I was strong enough to tackle the day for my children. My cousin (or my brother, as I call him) sees my pic on WhatsApp and decides to come to see me. He is very close to me and I adore him to pieces. He is a God sent angel to me. He came over and dropped off many gift cards worth a couple of thousand dollars. I felt bad for taking them, but he still left them. After that, he would chat with me by text telling me to pray more and detach myself from the world. He would ask how I was and I would say I was okay.

One day he scolded me and said, "Sister, why are you not in bliss? You're always saying I am okay. You say, 'I am good!'" But I wasn't "good" because it wasn't coming from within. I remember my sister would ask, "Did you take your medication?" My panic was so bad that It felt like I ran a marathon and I was gasping for air for 45 minutes. I would hide in my closet and cry for hours; never in front of the kids. I lost 48 lbs. from September 2019 to the end of December 2019.

In January 2020 I got Pneumonia. I was in so much physical and internal pain. I couldn't leave my bedroom for at least 3 weeks. I went to the hospital as I was throwing up with fevers and chills. I drove myself, stopping the car along the way to throw up. I didn't think that I should call an ambulance and the 10-15 minute drive felt never-ending. Once I get there. They took me straight in and put me on IV fluids. My glucose level was through the roof.

From 2017 to mid-June, 2020 I would go to the hospital multiple times because my glucose was too high. My sodium level dropped so significantly that my fingers and hands couldn't open and I had ketoacidosis. Every 2 weeks I landed in the emergency room at the hospital to get sodium through an IV. From 2017 onwards, my sugar levels are so bad that I had to see people at the diabetes complex care unit. They had social workers who saw me. I went through a check-up trying to figure out why my sugars were so high. They kept cranking my insulin up. They would have me sit in a room, giving me insulin until my sugar level went up. After 45 minutes, they injected me with more and again it's still sky-high. Crazy isn't it? Then they would send me home with no real answers. Now, I have to take 210 Units of Insulin 6 times a day. I am taking so many meds. Here are a few of them: Amitriptyline, Escitalopram, Lorazepam, Diclofenac, Naproxen, Hydromorphone, Cyclobenzaprine, Lenoltec No 2, Meloxicam and Pantoprazole Magnesium.

Despite all those medications, everything continued to get worse for me. Appointment after appointments but no cure other than suppressed emotions. I had no one to share my feelings with. Internally I was dying with guilt, resentment and wanting love and care from others. I love everyone. I think someone should be taking care of me but I had no one. I felt blind in my mind and my eyes were useless in seeing any blessings.

Fast forward to July 2020, where the world was in the middle of a pandemic and for that reason, 2020 was a bad year for many people. However, this was my turning point and happened to be the best year ever for me. By July 2020 I had become a brand new person with new hopes and new goals. As you read this book, you will discover my journey from darkness to light and full transformational healing.

My one big promise to you is that when you read this book, you will not only discover how you can also experience true healing no matter where you are or how dark things may seem. You will learn steps to heal not only yourself but generations of your family as well. You will learn to heal your relationship with yourself, your kids and your spouse. You will fulfill all your desires. Also, you will know that you are not alone in your current situation. You will learn all of the following and more:

> **How to Overcome emotional abuse**
> **How to Overcome physical, verbal, mental and financial abuse**
> **How to Avoid medication abuse to keep the status quo.**
> **How to Alleviate Suicidal and depressive episodes**
> **How to Alleviate Panic attacks and anxiety.**
> **How to get rid of Physical infections and Physical Pain**

*I look forward to helping you on your own journey and helping you overcome a life of darkness and pain and come into a life of peace, happiness and blessings! Remember, life's a journey to be experienced…Live passionately!*

*Chapter 1*

## OVERTHINKING

One of the people I love the most in my life who I am never able to let go of leaves me. I am unable to gather myself and keep myself together. I am left in so much pain. Pain that is so bad that it travels through my entire body. I can no longer sit. I move and twist my wrists and feet at my ankles because the pain is so bad throughout my body. I have ongoing bronchitis and Pneumonia. Infections start to flare up on the surface of my legs, mouth, everywhere on my body. I started to lose so much of my hair on my head. The strands of hair would come out in bunches. I started going bald on the crown of my head. Everything was taking effect on a physical level from my head to toes.

stop thinking of what happened to me and why. I hardly slept. I would sleep only an hour through the night. I just keep thinking… *God why me? Why am I being punished? How am I going to handle everything? God. My finances, God, my children, God, food, clothing and shelter for kids, God, my bills? How will I do it God? I have a big mountain to carry on my shoulders. How will I do this? How?* Yet, I was doing all this, all by myself since 2012. I never saw it. I think it was all about the stories we tell ourselves. I would always think that I was a very ugly person. As a kid, I remember being told I was ugly. I felt like a big fat zero. I grew up believing it. I thought no one wanted me. My parents, siblings, spouse, and one day my kids will never need me. I had no friends to associate with. I left all of them when I got married. Never thought of reuniting with them. I would see them at the malls here and there and would hide. I would think about what they would think of me. My self-image was so poor. They looked so cool just like they used to be in high school. All up to date in the latest clothing and style. I was just a basic person with no changes other than being married and having children. I had so many problems going on. I would hide so people didn't know what I was going through.

I reunited on Facebook in June 2020 with a few of my friends when one of my high school friends committed suicide. She left behind a 4-year-old daughter. No one knew what happened. Yes, she may have shown signs as she used to post some pics here and there about being in prison in her mind. I always thought she was happy. Always dressed up and posting pics with family and being happy. I lost my mind after that. I couldn't feel anything for myself or vision anything anymore. I always thought I was a positive person doing everything in a timely manner. Working, cooking, cleaning. I did all my responsibilities. I felt the future was just so dark for me. The good thing that happened was that I started to have my friends back on Facebook. I learned that they were going through similar problems as I was. I was like, "Oh my God!!! I always thought their life was better than mine!" It made me realize that I wasn't alone in this. Still, there were pieces breaking apart. I would try to hide my sadness from my children and cry in the shower for long periods of time. I had read that taking a shower reduces stress. Not for me. It was just getting worse. I would look at the flowing river in my backyard. Hearing it flow, I would say, "God, please take my pain away in the flowing river. I can't take it anymore."

Months go by… I am worse… I can barely cook anymore.

My mom and aunt call the priest from the temple home. Get a prayer done for the well-being of yourself and your kids. He is in shock to see the condition I am in; that a tall and healthy girl like me is in such a different state from where I was when he saw me a few years ago. He gives me a prayer to recite. **(all that is dried up will become green once again).**

*Ga-orhee Mehlaa 5 (**ANG 191**) GURU GRANTH SAHIB*

**Gauree, Fifth Mehl:**

sookay haray kee-ay khin maahay

**The dried branches are made green again in an instant.**

Amrit darisat sanch jeevaa-ay.

**His Ambrosial Glance irrigates and revives them.**

kaatay kasat pooray gurdayv.

**The Perfect Divine Guru has removed my sorrow.**

sayvak ka-o deenee apunee sayv. Rahaa-o.

**He blesses His servant with His service. |Pause|**

mit ga-ee chint punee man aasaa.

**Anxiety is removed, and the desires of the mind are fulfilled,**

karee da-i-aa satgur guntaasaa.

**when the True Guru, the Treasure of Excellence, shows His Kindness.**

dukh naathay sukh aa-ay samaa-ay.

**Pain is driven far away, and peace comes in its place**

dheel na paree jaa gur furmaa-ay.

**there is no delay, when the Guru gives the Order.**

ichh punee pooray gur milay.

**Desires are fulfilled, when one meets the True Guru**

naanak tay jan sufal falay.

**O Nanak, His humble servant is fruitful and prosperous.**

He says to me to leave all my other prayers for now and only do this. One morning, he sees I am not capable of sitting because I'm in so much pain. I start the prayer. I get healed from pneumonia, but I'm still in internal, physical pain. He tells me to let go of all my negative thoughts. What you want isn't going to happen for a few years, which was getting my family back together. I was so shattered, like broken pieces of glass. I try to fix it in my mind. I was hurting myself more. I felt as if I was picking up a piece of glass and it was giving me cuts. I was bleeding awfully. I can't sleep. Palpitations wake me up at 1 am. I cry and can't breathe because of panic. I gasp for breath and it takes at least 45 minutes for me to catch my breath. I have been getting up every day since, for a few years now, at 3 am and praying every day. Now, I cannot pray anymore because my stress level is so high. I try, but I cannot even hold the bible. My left arm aches and my chest hurts so much. The pain is so unbearable. It penetrates my body. Drop, by drop, it feels it's still going through my wrists, neck, ankles and full body. I start to cling to my bed more and more.

Finally, I am starting to feel that I need help. How can I free myself from being trapped? I have been trying to speak with God for the last few days to ask for help. I say, "God, please don't take my prayers away. You have taken everything from me. I only have your prayers." I am blaming everything on God. I don't see or feel that. I ask God, "Please clear my mind from overthinking—I'm tired." Then I say a prayer in Punjabi.

# Overthinking

# F A I T H

For some reason, I kept repeating this even through the night. I fell asleep doing it.

*Bilaaval, Fifth Mehl:( ANG 819-16) GURU GRANTH SAHIB*

*taatee vaa-o na lag-ee paarbarahm sarnaa-ee.*

**The hot wind does not even touch one who is under the Protection of the Supreme Lord God.**

*cha-ugirad hamaarai raam kaar dukh lagai na bhaa-ee.*

**On all four sides I am surrounded by the Lord's Circle of Protection; pain does not afflict me, O** *Siblings of Destiny. satgur pooraa bhayti-aa jin banat banaa-ee.*

**I have met the Perfect True Guru, who has done this deed.**

*raam naam a-ukhaDh dee-aa aykaa liv laa-ee. rahaa-o.*

**He has given me the medicine of the Lord's Name, and I enshrine love for the One Lord.**

*raakh lee-ay tin rakhanhaar sabh bi-aaDh mitaa-ee.*

**The Savior Lord has saved me, and eradicated all my sickness.**

*kaho naanak kirpaa bha-ee parabh bha-ay sahaa-ee.*

**Says Nanak, God has showered me with His Mercy; He has become my help and support.**

## *Chapter 2*

## LET IT HURT UNTIL IT CAN'T HURT ANYMORE

That night, I felt like I had been submerged in a deep, dark body of water; like the ocean on a dark night… only my hand is out. This is when someone comes in the boat… They are here to save me. They are telling me that they are here to help me. "Hold my hand!!" I grasp that hand. They pull me out of the dark oceans. I am in tears as I write this line. Here is where I *do* start believing that God works through people.

When we are no longer able to change a situation, we are challenged to change ourselves. I tried to smile on the outside—It was a lie. I was hiding so much pain inside. I couldn't smile at all. It was as if someone had stolen it. Days go by... I am in pretty bad shape. Here comes the life saver for me...

Finally, I see a video on Instagram by a person named Ranj Hothi. She was talking about a client that she had worked with. This client had mental health issues. I have known Ranj since elementary school. We never communicated. I didn't even know I followed her on Facebook and Instagram since 2009. She was glowing and radiant. I first commented that she looked beautiful. Then I thought, *Wait a minute. She is saying something.* I deleted the comment. I started to watch the video and began to feel like she could be the one to help me. I wasn't ready to talk to CMAH (The Centre for Addiction and Mental Health is Canada's largest mental health teaching hospital dealing with mental crisis). I wasn't mental. I was in a deep depression.

For some reason, I sent a direct message to her. I texted her saying, "I need to talk to you. Can you please call me?" She said she was busy, but she would. I waited until the second day and messaged her again. She finally called me on the third day and I told her what I was going through; that I needed some help. Ranj spoke with me for almost two and a half hours. I connected so well with her. She tells me about the program. It costs a lot of money and I have some doubt for a split second, but I decided to join using my Visa.

The first thing she did was make me write an affirmation. I wrote it. It felt like magic how I became at ease. I wrote that I know this anxiety will fade away like a flowing river. Then I wrote that however big the mountain is, I can climb it. It just felt so good. I felt light just writing that. She sends me the outline, contract and access to the 12 lessons.

The next morning before I started my lesson I wrote a letter to God first. I wrote, *My loving Guru ji (LORD), Please enlighten what's dark in me. Strengthen what is weak in me. Mend what is broken in me. Bind what's bruised in me. Heal what's sick in me. And lastly, Revive whatever peace and love has died in me. The beautiful soul that belongs to the Supreme Lord. I have your light and strength in me. Please guide me. Thank you, God, for everything. Regards, Rosie Kaur.*

For once I felt I wasn't blaming. Now, I will tell you that my story is a great example of a person who is ignorant of beliefs, faith, trust, or I should say, gratitude and what happens when you have gratitude in yourself or life. I didn't know what gratitude was or what being grateful was. I knew from when I was a kid to say thank you to people, but that was it. That's the way we are all programmed. So, the first week into the program, I doubted it. I asked Ranj, "Does this work? I had paid so much for it." She told me to join the group. There were, I think, six of us in the group. Everyone reached out and texted to do the work and you will see your results. I kid you not, the seventh day I felt a huge shift. As everything had brightened up for me. I went from dying to living mode—like flowers coming back to life.

# Let It Hurt Until It Can't Hurt Anymore

In the first lesson I learned what my beliefs were, and how I changed, and became all positive. Then setting BIG goals. I didn't know what my goals were when I joined. I thought goals were tiny things we need. I started setting BIG goals and I started to achieve them.

A goal is something you want to grow with. I learned the importance of setting both personal and business goals. I started to feel like I was going to set something on fire. I started gaining my energy back.

I would recommend that you don't listen to anyone who tells you it's not possible. I now realize that anything is possible in your life. I want to inspire you. I want you to approach this book thinking about your current mindset. What kind of mindset do you have? Do you have a **Growth mindset**? This is where you think, *I can learn anything I want to, and when I'm frustrated I persevere because when I fail, I learn.* Or do you have a **Fixed mindset**? This is where you think, *When I fail,*

*I give up. I don't like to be challenged and I don't like to try in fear that I may fail.*

Mindset is everything. As Henry Ford once said, "Whether you think you can, or you think you can't—you're right." Remember this.

Let me tell you that MENTAL ILLNESS is NOT...

- A choice
- Attention seeking
- An insult or an adjective
- Something you can snap out of
- A crime
- A weakness
- A flaw character
- Laziness
- Fake or all in their head
- An excuse
- Funny or a joke
- Trendy or cool
- Just a phase
- Discriminative (it can affect anybody)
- The same for everyone
- Less important than other illnesses

*Chapter 3*

# LIFE IS GETTING UP AN HOUR EARLY TO LIVE AN HOUR MORE

Going forward, just learning that we often have unconscious awareness about a lot of things. We just start doing things. Our world looks different when we change our thinking. New ways start to show up. Results start to get different and better. It's our behavior that we need to change. Why do you behave like this? It's a habit that we have to change; a habit that we have carried since we were kids. We were conditioned. We have to change that. How are you programmed? It's the power of habit and the subconscious mind. Environment is more important for the conscious mind. Energy flows through and to us. We think. Paradigms cause us to act the way we do. We make decisions that are not proper. We are not conscious. Internalize the thinking and the behavior and the thinking will change.

After two weeks into the program, I am so positive that I am starting to feel light in my body. I started to finally walk a bit. Little by little I am getting better physically. The pain is starting to subside a bit. I am getting back on track to waking up at 3 am to do my prayers, lessons, and go out for a walk. I start to forget all the pain I ever had. Then my new affirmations came in which I started to write that I have financial freedom, abundance and prosperity. For the first time I felt, I am debt-free and that I had all the money I always needed. My relationship with my kids was improving. Instead of feeling overwhelmed and exhausted, I started to feel energetic. The ugliness I felt within me faded. I felt like I was the most beautiful woman out there. I started to feel so happy, joyful and calm. I had to let go. I also learned with the lesson how to do the things that I wasn't applying methods too. I had to let go of the thought of my significant other leaving me, leaving me with debt, the business, the house, kids, etc. Forgetting that I had debt or had anybody in my life. If I didn't, I would've still been stuck. I am so happy within myself. I am in high spirits. I survived because the fire inside me burned brighter than the fire around me.

*Gratitude helps you see what's there instead of what isn't*

I am Grateful that I made it in life. I'm alive. I am so grateful for everything. I have so much gratitude watching the sunrise. It's the little things that are big for me now. My results were so enormous. It felt like I had a magic wand or there was a genie commanding me and making my wishes come true. I had so much bliss. Everything was coming true. I was changing big time. I had so much energy that I felt like I was 16 again.

Just being happy and grateful changed my life tremendously. I went from depression, panic and anxiety to a joyful fulfilling life. I learned how our logical thinking changes our surroundings. How we change our thinking.

*Chapter 4*

## I'M SLOWLY BECOMING THE PERSON I SHOULD HAVE BECOME A LONG TIME AGO

I feel that life is so magical. I am so happy that my family has seen the change in me. People notice how changed I am. My doctor, neighbors, friends and all. Even my son's friend asked if there is something different with me. I say, "What do you think it is?" He couldn't figure it out, but said something has definitely changed. I was once a person who didn't know how to apply makeup properly or be in style and dress up, but now, I'm doing it all! I get ready so quickly. I feel beautiful within myself. I went on shopping sprees for myself for the first time in my life. I learned that I have to prioritize myself in this lesson. Everything feels so light within me when everything is flowing to me with ease. I feel like I am shining from within. Radiant like a diamond. I feel there is a bright yellow aura around me.

It is here I learned about our self-image. I learned that we tend to look outside for our image. We have two kinds of images. One is where we walk, talk and dress; look good on the outside. The second is the internal image of ourselves. This is spiritual Image. We hardly ever go from the inside image to the outside image. Most of us are more cautious about the outside image. I would like to say that our image is what we think or about our internal thoughts; that's the way we show up on the outside. If we change our internal thoughts, we change our external image to positivity and attraction. From feeling ugly and low always, I was playing victim to the new me. I was now Healthy, pain-free and happy within myself.

My brother is so delighted to see me change. His one sister who used to say, "I am okay," when asked, now says, "I am in Chardikala (bliss) and full of gratitude." It's so beautiful to be full of the laughter and happiness that I lost completely about four years ago. I am completely off my anti-anxiety and panic pills, which I had been taking for years. If I recall, it was 21 years that I took these meds. NOW, I have naturally healed myself. Let me tell you that falling in love with yourself is the first secret to happiness.

### *Self-love, Self-image and Self-care*

This is where I figure out, "Shit, I was a darn people pleaser… HOLY SHIT!" I never used to care about my health. I would host parties. I would cook, prepare appetizers, and meals all night, all alone. Clean during the day with the help of my kids getting the house ready for the guests. I would do things for people even though one part of my body would want to say no. I was pushing myself to the extremes. I didn't realize it. Do you know why pleasing people isn't a positive? It had a negative force in me. The positive force kept saying, "No, watch your body." I kept pushing it. Whether I had kids or had surgeries. I was up in the kitchen cooking as soon as I got home. I would tell myself, *No one cares or loves me. They are not here for me.* That wasn't the case. It was me not loving myself and caring for myself. I was always overwhelmed, depressed and exhausted. I never gave time to myself. Now I learned that I should be caring and loving to myself first. I have become happy being alone with myself. I also am so strong in my mind, body and soul.

*Chapter 5*

# The Law of Attraction Is This—You Don't Attract What You Want, You Attract What You Are. Be the Person You Want to Attract!

**Beliefs and Goals**: We tend to live from the outside in when we should be living from the inside out. We have 5 senses, which are: see, hear, smell, taste and touch. Then, as human beings, we are equipped with higher mental faculties: Perception, Will, Imagination, Memory, Reason and Intuition. That's actually a total of 6 mental faculties. A lot of people are not aware of these senses. I learned that repetition is key and that it reflects on the subconscious mind. We use reflection to learn to make a connection between what we are taught and what we know.

Basically, I would say that thoughts create things. Careful what you think and do.

The goals that I manifested came true. I started earning $8,000 a month. My belief becomes so strong that all of my goals are turning into reality. I have a job from home working with Medevac as an ambulance dispatcher. We transfer patients worldwide. That's a job my brother provided. I would never in my wildest dreams think that my family would give me a job or I would be working with them. I am getting the $8,000 a month I need to run the house and I am not working crazy hard. Everything is just flowing. Life has become peaceful. There is no such thing as debt in my life anymore. As they say, do not resist change. Let everything flow. Everything is amazing for me. I learned what fear or a habit was. We back up and lean and hold onto fear when we are growing. It is where we stay comfortable and can't get out of our comfort zone. It is also a self-image we create for ourselves. When we feel growth, that's when we are going to have a quantum leap. You see yourself doing what you want by stepping out of the box or your comfort zone.

The belief system is based upon what we evaluate of something and frequently if we re-evaluate what happens to us. If you keep a belief in a certain thing and can't change it, it's habitual or overpowered by repetition. We can accomplish anything, but we have to believe it. The emotions or feelings that we feel set up the vibration inside us. Then vibration causes the action. The action will cause the reaction. That's where the results will show up. You have to hold the belief in you. In action, my life has become blissful. The scariest place to be is the same place you were last year—I decided and I grew. I finally started letting a lot of things slide. I saw what was in my control and what wasn't. Self-control is strength. Calmness is mastery. You have to get to a point where your mood doesn't drift based on the insignificant actions of others to control the direction of your life. Don't allow your emotions to empower your intelligence.

Another concept I want to share with you is called Quantum Leap. I am not sure if you have ever heard of Quantum Leap before, I hadn't until I became a coach. You may be asking yourself, "What is a Quantum leap?" A Quantum Leap is a huge, often sudden, increase or advance in something. A Quantum Leap requires **a quantum shift** in three areas: your mindset, your energy (how you feel, your emotions), and your actions. To collapse time and expedite your growth, step into the shoes of your future self who has already achieved the goal and start to embody her. A great book you can also read or reference to learn more about Quantum Leaps is called *You 2: A High Velocity Formula for Multiplying Your Personal Effectiveness in Quantum Leaps,* by Price Pritchett. In the book, the author explains this incredible strategy for achieving breakthrough performance which replaces the concept of attaining gradual, incremental success through massive effort. It puts forth 18 key components for building massive success while expending less effort. This concept has helped me immensely in my path to healing and growth and is something you may want to use as a tool for yourself on your journey!

*Chapter 6*

# YOU MAKE YOUR LIFE HARD BY ALWAYS BEING IN YOUR HEAD. LIFE IS SIMPLE. GET OUT OF YOUR HEAD AND GET INTO THE MOMENT.

Change your attitude. As attitude starts to flow different energies towards us, there is repetition that causes the change in us. Our body is a mass cell. We are vibrating constantly. We have to alter our attitude to make changes and attract things. If we are positive, we attract good things. If we are negative, we attract negativity. If we are mentally and physically in a bad vibration, we will attract it to us. The vibration is going to dictate what you attract. When we move into a positive vibration, we begin to attract energy to us. This is how we can keep control of ourselves. Our attitude is a composite of our thoughts, our feelings, and our actions. our thoughts, feelings and actions are energy that we send out into the universe. I changed my attitude.

When I lost all my excuses I found my results. I created financial freedom, abundance and prosperity in my life. I have abundant health and wealth. I have no stress about anything anymore. Everything is just flowing with ease. I am not worried about anything. The worry, doubt and fear have diminished. I surrender to the Grace upon me. I am so calm, like the ocean that cares for each wave until it reaches the shore. I am given so much help from the universe.

Back then, the scariest thing for me to think about was that one year from that point I would be in the same place I had been the past year, and so I grew. I changed dramatically in so many facets of my life. Everyone I met left them with an impression of increase. I started to say, "Hello" and "God bless you" to everyone I met. Whether this person was a child, adult, senior, cashier, doctor, nurse, etc. I even started to say, "God bless" to people's pets. I started to feel so good and light. I have outpouring love for all humanity now. I feel so much relaxation. I find that I am getting a lot of love from people in return. People tell me they can feel so much positivity from me and that they feel so good. I feel so rich. Just by making people happy by saying, "God bless."

I started to talk and spend time with seniors wherever I met them. They would feel bad that they were taking up my time. In me, I felt that they were lonely and needed someone to hear their stories. It felt so good just being a listening ear and blessing them. I remember their faces, a nice smile and they would look calm. I felt so amazed that I could actually be this kind of person. The feeling and joy in me increased day by day. I started to think that life was amazing. Let me tell you that the past has no power to stop you from being present in the now. Only your grievance about the past can do that. Grievance is the baggage of old thoughts and emotions that you don't let go of.

*Chapter 7*

## FORGIVENESS AND LETTING GO

I felt that my fear of anger, guilt and resentment would not teach me anything. Then I forgave myself and others. I used to always say, "Every day is a new day," to "Forgive and forget." I learned that in school when I was a child, but part of me didn't fully do it I think. That's where my guilt and resentment came from. I forgave everyone who was close to me from childhood to the point where I literally was crashing. Ranj taught our group to write forgiveness letters. I wrote to them in my journal. It felt so good. I had taken all the weight off my shoulders. Life evolved for me. I started to see the relationship with my family getting stronger with them.

I would like to ask you, "Do you know what forgiveness is?"

For me, forgiving is a feeling of understanding, empathy and compassion for the one who hurt you. Forgiving doesn't mean you forget or excuse the harm done to you or make up with the person who caused the harm. **Forgiveness brings a kind of peace that helps you go on with life,** so you don't take a toll on your mind. Forgiveness is about goodness, about extending mercy to those who've harmed us, even if they don't "deserve" it. It is not about finding excuses for the offending person's behavior or pretending it didn't happen. Neither is there a quick formula you can follow. Forgiveness is a process. But it's well worth the effort. Working on forgiveness can help us increase our self-esteem and give us a sense of inner strength and safety. It can reverse the lies that we often tell ourselves when someone has hurt us deeply. Lies like, *I am defeated* or *I'm not worthy*. Forgiveness heals us and allows us to move on in life with meaning and purpose. Forgiveness matters, and we will be its primary beneficiary.

Studies have shown that forgiving others produces strong psychological benefits for the one who forgives. It has been shown to decrease depression, anxiety, unhealthy anger, and the symptoms of PTSD (Post-traumatic stress disorder). But we don't just forgive to help ourselves. Forgiveness can lead to psychological healing. It is not something about you or done for you. It is something you extend toward another person, because you recognize, over time, that it is the best response to the situation. Forgiveness changes your inner world. You may come to this through religious beliefs or a humanist philosophy or even through your belief in evolution. It's important to cultivate this mindset of valuing our common humanity so that it becomes harder to discount someone who has harmed you as unworthy.

You can show love in small ways in everyday encounters; like smiling at a harried grocery cashier or taking time to listen to a child. Giving love when it's unnecessary helps to build the love muscle, making it easier to show compassion toward everyone. If you practice small acts of forgiveness and mercy—extending care when someone harms you—in everyday life, this too will help. Perhaps you can refrain from honking when someone cuts you off in traffic, or hold your tongue when your spouse snaps at you and extend a hug instead.

Sometimes pride and power can weaken your efforts to forgive by making you feel entitled and inflated so that you hang onto your resentment as a cause. Try to catch yourself when you are acting from that place, and choose forgiveness or mercy, instead.

It's important to figure out who has hurt you and how. Address your inner pain. This may seem that not every action that causes suffering is unjust. To become clearer, you can look carefully at the people in your life, for example, your parents, siblings, peers, spouse, co-workers, children, and even yourself and rate how much they've hurt you. Then acknowledge where or who the pain is coming from. There are many forms of emotional pain. For me, the worst ones were anxiety, depression, lack of trust, self-care, or low self-esteem. All of these can be addressed by forgiveness. So it's important to identify the kind of pain you are suffering from and to acknowledge it. The more pain you have, the more important it is to forgive, for the purpose of having emotional healing.

Scientists have studied what happens in the brain when we think about forgiving. They understand that when people successfully imagine forgiving someone (in a hypothetical situation) that people show healing and empathy. This tells us that empathy is connected to forgiveness. If you look into some of the details or reasons in the life of the person who harmed you, you can often see more clearly what wounds he/she carries and start to develop empathy for him/her. First, try to imagine him/her as an innocent child, needing love and support. Did he/she get that from their parents? There is research that shows that if an infant does not receive attention and love from primary caregivers then he/she will have a weak attachment. It damages trust.

It may prevent him/her from ever getting close to others and there is loneliness and conflict for the rest of his/her life.

You will be able to put the entire scenario together for the person who hurt you from early childhood through adulthood. You may be able to tell of his/her psychological suffering and begin to understand what you share. You may recognize him/her as a vulnerable person. A person who was wounded and is wounding in return. Despite what he/she may have done to hurt you, you realize that he/she did not deserve to suffer either.

Recognize that we all carry wounds in our hearts that can help open the door to forgiveness. We can forgive.

Some people may think that loving another person who's harmed you is not possible. But, I've found that many people who forgive eventually find a way to open their hearts. I am the biggest example of that!

For forgiveness I used to recite this prayer from the Holy Bible:

*Na Ko Bairi Nahi Bigana*

**I see No Stranger, I See No Enemy**

*kaanrhaa mehlaa 5. Sri Guru Granth Sahib:(1299 13-15)*

*Kaanraa, Fifth Mehl:*

*bisar ga-ee sabh taat paraa-ee.*

**I have totally forgotten my jealousy of others,**

*jab tay saaDhsangat mohi paa-ee. rahaa-o.*

**since I found the Saadh Sangat, the Company of the Holy. Pause**

*naa ko bairee nahee bigaanaa sagal sang ham ka-o ban aa-ee.*

**No one is my enemy, and no one is a stranger. I get along with everyone.**

*jo parabh keeno so bhal maani-o ayh sumat saaDhoo tay paa-ee.*

**Whatever God does, I accept that as good. This is the sublime wisdom I have obtained from the Holy.**

*sabh meh rav rahi-aa parabh aykai paykh paykh naanak bigsaa-ee.*

**The One God is pervading in all. Gazing upon Him, beholding Him, Nanak blossoms forth in happiness.**

## An Exercise to Help You in Your Journey

I want you to take a notebook and just write these seven emotional words: Clarity, Love, Courage, Appreciation, Strength, Freedom and Security. Then stay focused on them long enough that you will actually start to feel movement inside you. Your path will light up for you.

You want LOVE? Be Love.

You want LIGHT? Be Light.

You have all this within you. Just take a deep breath and feel it.

*Chapter 8*

## SOME JOURNEYS TAKE US FAR FROM HOME & SOME ADVENTURES LEAD US TO OUR DESTINY

When things started to become great for me I realized that my problems are so tiny compared to others. I didn't even notice that I had a lot of gratitude. You can too. What matters is how quickly you do what your soul directs.

Loving ourselves is feminist intervention. It is choosing to care for one's own bodies and lives as a priority in all of our various labors— Making a life, raising a family. We can care for ourselves by remembering our purpose of who we are. We can inhale, breathe through energy and power into our bodies and we exhale through fear and pain. We become our best selves, healing with forgiveness and reconciliation.

Like a lotus, I went through so much. Lotus signifies a flower. We too have the ability to rise from the mud, bloom out of darkness and radiate into the world.

Like the moon, we must go through phases of emptiness to feel full again. It was a phase from darkness to light that I took. I have the spiritual divine light within me today. The feeling is so beautiful. Full of joy and excitement every day.

Today, I have a vision. It was an effective vision of what kind of work I wanted to do. The knowledge I have I want to give to others. I now own my mind. I have awareness. I have clients. By helping them heal, I am in joy, abundance and prosperity. I have to have a great attitude. I find the good in everyone. I feel an outpouring of love for all. I understand what people are going through. I help them in that way so they are able to let go. I have to lead them with a good attitude. I am grateful for this. Thanking the universe every moment I get. I have the grace of the Lord upon me and my family. I have faith, trust and belief in who I have become and what is coming to me. *Now that I have mastered Survival Mode, I am free like a butterfly and it's time to live and fly. My hope for you is that you experience the same love, light and freedom on your own journey wherever that may take you. God bless you all and remember…*

**Life is a journey to be experienced…**

# Conclusion & Resources

**To you:** *Remember that you are loved just as you are. You are worthy of this earth and its seas and skies. And for the gifts, it has to be offered to you just as you are. And the earth will receive all the gifts that you give it as long as they are gifts given by you with joy. Let joy in every day!*

My mission or goal for 2022 and beyond is to heal as many people as I can. As they say, "God works through people." I have a purpose for being here now. I see it so clearly. I want to heal humanity. People going through tough times, I am here for you all and would love to connect with you anytime.

Now that you have read this book, what kind of mindset do you have NOW?

**Growth mindset**: I can learn anything I want to and when I'm frustrated I persevere—when I fail I learn.

**Fixed mindset**: When I fail I give up—I don't like to be challenged.

**Decide…**

Is this the life you want to live?

Is this the person you want to love?

Is this the best version you can be?

Can you be stronger, kinder and more compassionate?

Breathe in and breathe out and decide.

Let me tell you this, God gives everyone a gift. It's up to us to discover what that gift is for us, how to use it, and how to make it grow.

You CAN go from nothing to everything! Just like I did, "From nothing to something, to everything and I can help you do just that."

I am so happy and grateful now that I have friends around the world who have crossed my path and who have helped me and shaped me into who I am today. There is a reason for everything. I see it with clarity now. I thank my family, friends and everyone else for being a part of my journey. God bless

**If you or someone you know would like additional life coaching or resources for creating new desired results and full transformation of your life, you can book a free 20-minute consultation here with Rosie: www.calendly.com/healingwithin. On this call, we will discuss where you are, where you are looking to go and we will map out a plan to get you there. You can also visit www.RosieKaur.com**

# About The Author

## Rosie Kaur

As a primary caregiver to my family, I never anticipated progress in life and barely survived as I managed ongoing anxiety, bronchitis, pneumonia and depression. However at my initial turning point, I discovered Bob Proctor's teachings and discovered the connection disease has to your body and was able to remove every last ounce of disease from my own body. For the first time in my life, I had no stress about what my responsibilities were and allowed the universe to guide me. I wouldn't be here today if it was not for my persistence and determination of my inner being.

Today I am a coach to those who are ready to free themselves from the grasp of their limited minds. Today I dream of the life I deserve and work every day to make it come to fruition for myself and my clients.A portion of all profits from the sales of this book will be going to Women's Groups and shelters to help others who were on the same path I was at one time.

I have been on a journey for more than 40 years now with this woman.

I have allowed her to be broken and shattered.

I have allowed others to treat her with disrespect and abuse her.

I have allowed her to fight for others who won't even stand for her.

I've seen her struggle in pain.

I saw her cry.

## About The Author

I saw her beat herself up.

I've watched her forgive others without hesitation and love them again.

She has put her trust & belief in people, who have never loved or believed in her.

I saw her see the good in others, even when they didn't see it in themselves.

I saw her give love & compassion to everyone… Except for herself.

I saw her fall many times & STAND BACK UP SO MANY TIMES, trying to keep her strength and ground.

I saw her trying multiple times to be a bright shining light for the world.

I saw her love others unconditionally despite all she went through.

I have stood paralyzed by fear, while she bravely fought battles in her mind, heart and soul like a warrior.

*I am in tears writing this.*

This woman has made many bad choices along the way. Of course, she is not perfect, and she reminds herself of that fact often.

She has a fiery temper if she's mad. As much as she wants to give up she is stubborn to keep going and keep up on anything that she believes in. If she loves you, she will fight to the death for you. She is trustworthy and true.

Some love this woman, some like her, and some don't care for her at all.

She has tried many times to do the right thing in her life.

Every mistake, failure, trial, disappointment, struggle, success, joy, and achievement has shaped her into who she is today.

This woman is God's WARRIOR.

She's not perfect.

She is unstoppable, broken many times, but beautifully standing with strength.

*She signifies love.*

*She signifies life.*

*She signifies hope.*

*She is a transformation.*

*She is brave.*

*She is balanced.*

*She will never stop learning, growing or moving forward.*

*She... is me.*

*Nanak Nam Chard Kala Teray Bhanay Sarbaat Da Bhalla*

***In the name of the Divine Oneness, we find ever-rising high spirits,***

***Within your will, may there be grace for all of Humanity***

# TESTIMONIALS

*"Rosie made the decision and took the actions to change her life in profound ways. It is an honour and privilege to have been part of her journey as she stepped into her shine as beautifully as she does."*

**Ranj Hothi**

*"Rosie truly understands the darkness of pain and trauma. The way she crawled herself out of a poverty mindset, from despair and misery to be able to help herself and her six children is undeniably heroic. Her heart's true love and passion is to help others do the same and the love, light and support is going to transform the world."*

**Selene Bartolo**

*"Rosie has found a way to combine spiritual compassion with intellectual compassion. It is clearly evident that she has written and delivered this journey with her soul. Her understanding and empathy are clearly felt and seen throughout this beautifully choreographed guided journey."*

**Christine Mattingly**

*"Rosie is a beautiful soul who spreads positivity, love and compassion around her surroundings. My husband and I are inspired by her and her courage to fight negativity. Her thoughts about happiness and manifestation are pervasive and persuasive. She was an angel who guided and supported us to overcome our anxiety about settling in a new country and being new parents. With love her strong, mindful, passionate and full of life personality and we love her."*

**Priyanka Thakkar & Nayan Thakkar**

# THANK YOU FOR READING MY BOOK!

## DOWNLOAD YOUR FREE GIFTS

### Read This First

Just to say thanks for buying and reading my book, I would like to give you a few free bonus gifts, no strings attached!

### To Download Now, Visit:

http://www.healingwithrosie.com/freegift

*I appreciate your interest in my book, and I value your feedback as it helps me improve future versions of this book. I would appreciate it if you could leave your invaluable review on Amazon.com with your feedback. Thank you!*

www.ingramcontent.com/pod-product-compliance
Lightning Source LLC
Chambersburg PA
CBHW070952180426
43194CB00042B/2468